DAS NEW BOOK II

1. The girls

pictures from nice cuties are good for connecting people.

2. Yeppa

What would you think of ehe combination between two languages

That's true and the way for connecting people. Beginning to play but the next step is a new art of font. The process will begin with development of font which contains all like Arabic and Chinese etc unit for the script -

Since childhood Mr. Feiler had a special type which some people say that they think of Egypt. Some people have the opinion it could be a program but who had developed this and why he knew about - it's amazing that a hand writing program app for smart phone shows Chinese characters of fonts

The translation giving right text.

3. Waiting

Really bad ☐ ☐

Sitting and using this for writing

With app of smartphones naturally it is one with the function save as. Damning where saved? Hmm well yeppa llol

Saved in the program

The consequences are: Copy. Using the following possibility either copy to a external text online or sending by self address. At home wlan outside Wi-Fi what's the difference? The bites/second.

4. Waiting part two

The factor getting tired □ □through writing. The light is artificial the eyes with pain. A little bit theatrical

It doesn't matter. Hopefully saved

5. The X

First listen again to the music. The own office programm is a challenge – because the difference between selection. Making changes like the language from german to english – or from english to german. The text is paint with red colour without changing.

6. Time for Pictures

Mrs. Feiler had the opitnion, that its time to show more images. Here some of them:

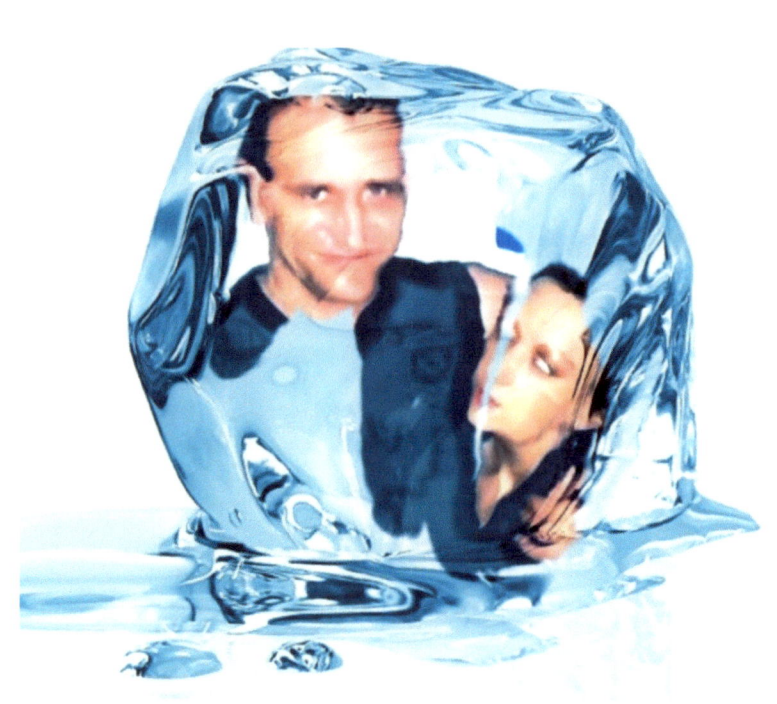

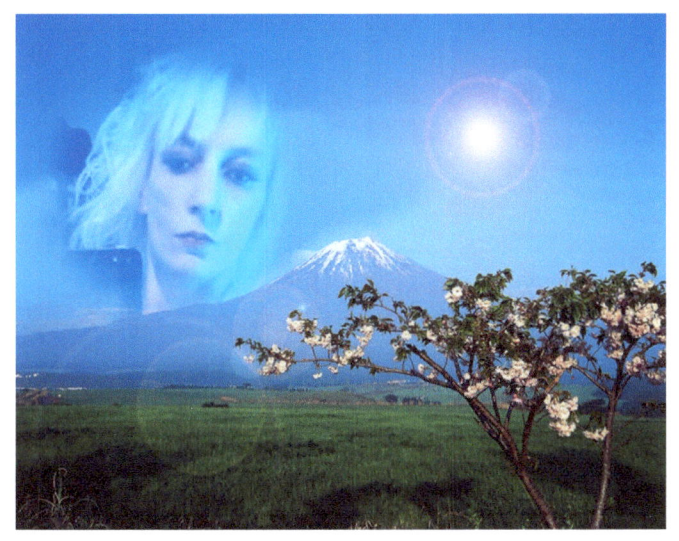

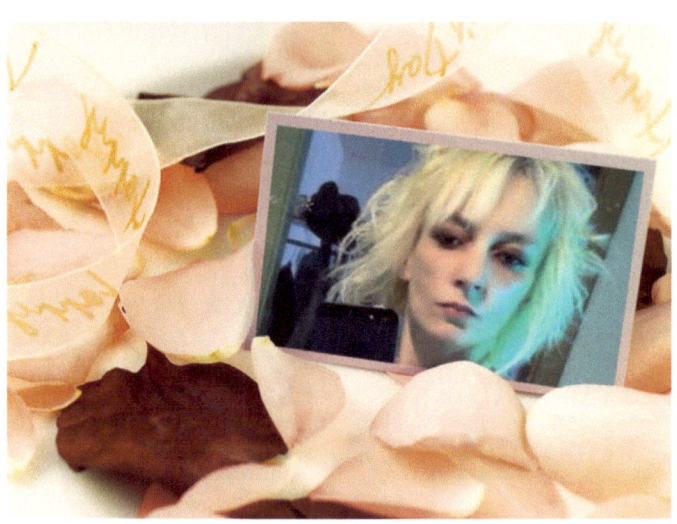

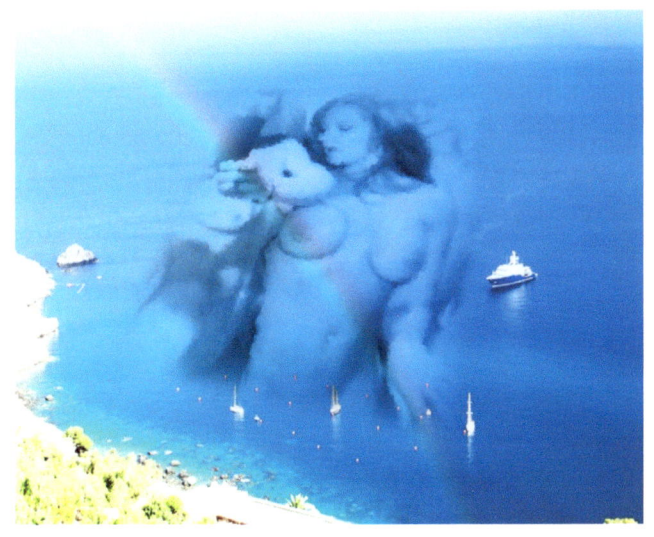

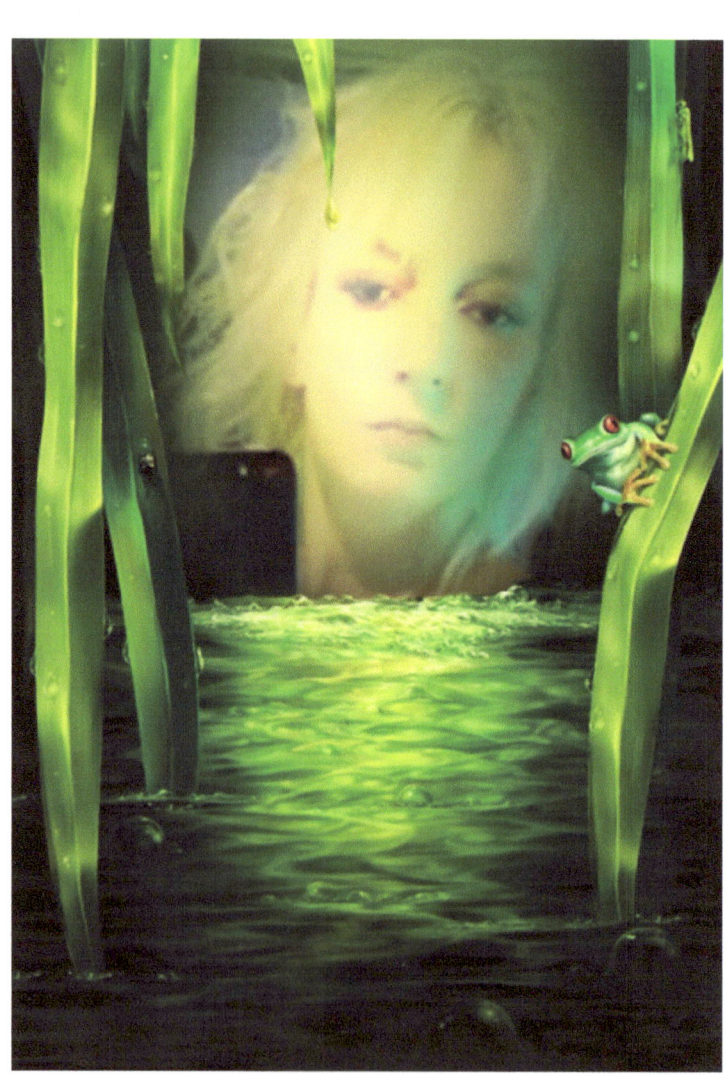

7. China and the Smog

China is a strange country. There is a place, called Place of heavently peace where people were shot. The Air is full of Smog, but a Model Agency had the idea to use the respiratory protection masks for fashion – the models have the respiratory protection mask in the face in the same colour as the clothing. And that is a success. Beautiful models who have to cough after work – Maybe they can indeed use the utensils after work. Health Care like in the USA -

Mrs. Feller has known since childhood personally Chinese, so to speak, grew up with different nationalities. The mentality is strange - but as a child, not a problem. The hair of Chinese girls grow faster. This news came on the radio today

8. unn ∩u?

Thats the question. Time for Images

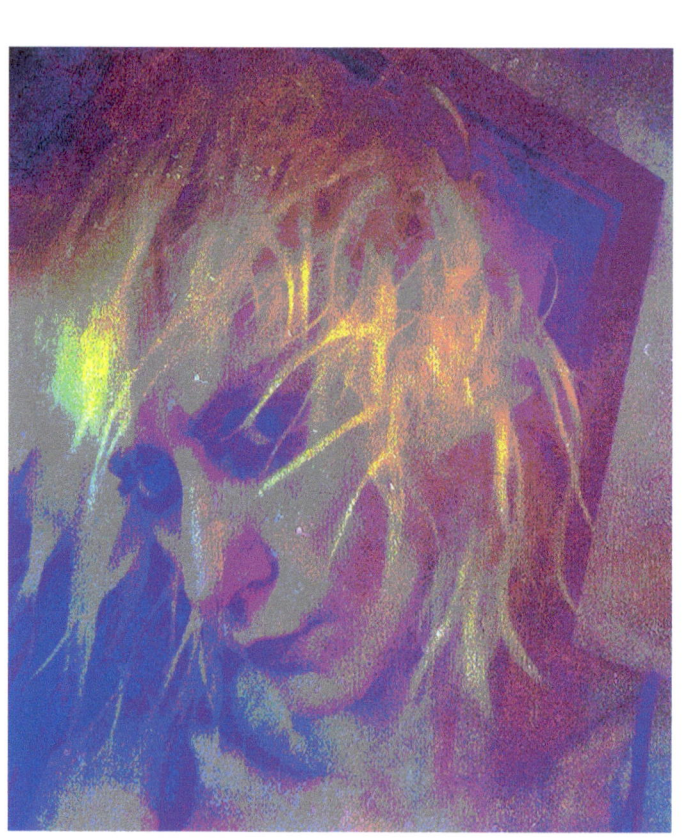

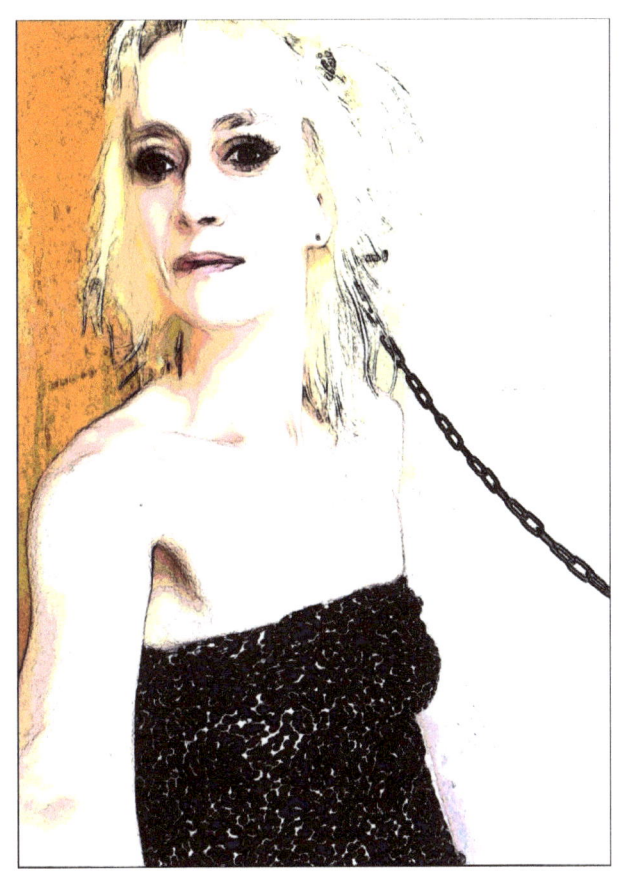

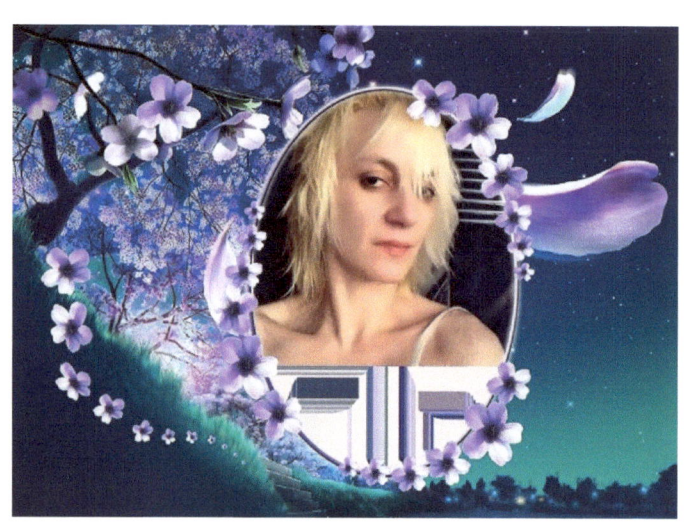

8. Do you know Flash Player?

Flash Player for Smartphones are the hell. Like the human being, who is responsible for USB Stick or Lan. A lot of Apps with Discription, but where is the link to download? The net gives informations about answers by user, but where is the download? Today it seems that for Lumia with the operating system win 8.1 there is no app. But for a special program I need a update - Flash Player - and now? I am angry and its time for a image.

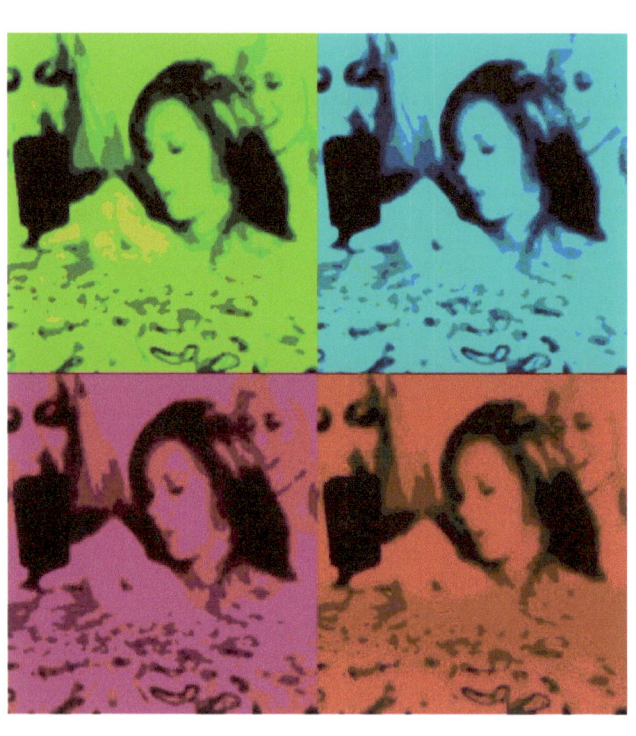

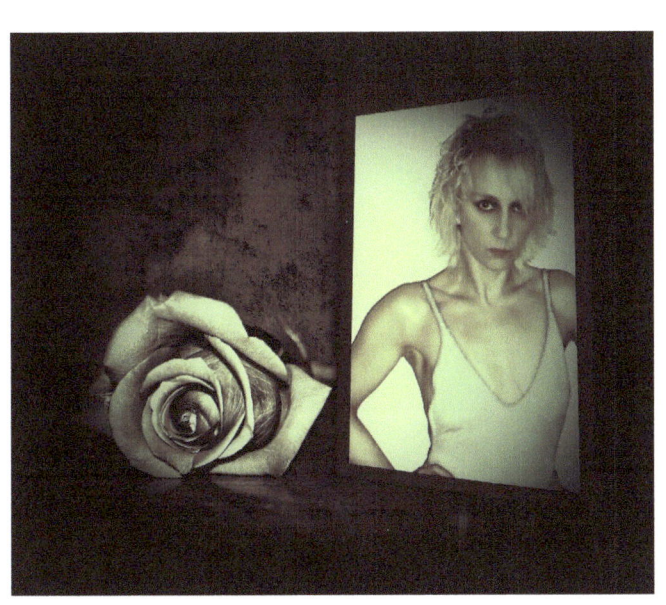

Dont forget to sing the Yeppa and Cutiesongs!